Four Winds of Revelation

Kenneth Cox

Pacific Press®
Publishing Association
Nampa, Idaho | Oshawa, Ontario, Canada
www.pacificpress.com

D0546742

Cover design by Gerald Lee Monks
Cover design resources from iStockphoto.com
Inside design by Aaron Troia

Additional copies of this book are available by calling toll-free
1-800-765-6955 or by visiting http://www.adventistbookcenter.com.

ISBN 13: 978-0-8163-5884-7
ISBN 10: 0-8163-5884-2

July 2015

Table of Contents

Introduction

Today we see floods in parts of our world that have never experienced flooding before, covering up cars, filling homes with mud and water, and sweeping away everything in their paths. At the same time, large areas experience fires that can take weeks to bring under control. The soil cries out for water because of drought; while in other places, numerous homes and great swaths of forests are burned. Elsewhere, tornadoes turn entire communities into rubble in a matter of seconds. Each year, the toll taken by natural disasters seems to be worse than the year before.

Why? What is happening? Even elderly people are saying, "I have never witnessed anything like this before." The Bible gives us insight into what is taking place.

"You, LORD, in the beginning laid the foun-
  dation of the earth,
And the heavens are the work of Your hands.
They will perish, but You remain;
And they will all grow old like a garment"
  (Hebrews 1:10, 11).

Yes, the earth is growing old. Humankind is de-
stroying the fragile ecosystem that God put in
place to protect the world.

In Revelation 11:18, God warns humankind
that He will "destroy those who destroy the
earth." The winds of strife are beginning to
blow across our world. The apostle John wrote,
"After these things I saw four angels standing
at the four corners of the earth, holding the
four winds of the earth, that the wind should
not blow on the earth, on the sea, or on any
tree" (Revelation 7:1). Verses 2 and 3 speak
of the four winds having power to harm the
earth. In Bible prophecy, the wind is used to
represent war, strife, and destruction (Jeremiah
51:1; Daniel 7:2). Although Revelation 7 does
not specifically define what these "four winds"
are, it does state that they will harm the earth.

Introduction

And I believe we can apply them to four categories of things I see happening today that are harming, and will continue to harm, the earth and its people. These four categories are (1) the Wind of Natural Disasters, (2) the Wind of Change, (3) the Wind of Force, and (4) the Wind of Compromise.

Let's examine each of these areas and see what they tell us about the world we live in today and what lies ahead.

Chapter 1

The Wind of Natural Disasters

In the early 1900s, when the earth's population started to multiply at an alarming rate, people began to realize that the population was beginning to outstrip the food supply. However, to put more land into the production of food required tilling and seeding more soil. Back then, humankind was limited to draft animals and turning plows. But the invention of the tractor arrived just in time, enabling farmers to plant as much acreage as they possessed. In addition, the mining of phosphate and the production of petroleum by-products made fertilizer plentiful and cheap; its increased use enabled farmers to grow bigger and better crops. As a result, by the 1940s farming was being done on a large scale, food was plentiful, and the birth rate accelerated.

I grew up on a farm in Oklahoma. Walking down a country road one day, I noticed that the corn on one side of the road was larger, greener, and taller than the corn on the other side of the road. I just assumed one farmer had fertilized more effectively than the other. However, I soon noticed a sign on a fencepost near the field of larger corn. The sign stated, "Hybrid Number PO157." I subsequently learned that the genetic structure of the plant had been changed to make it larger, greener, and taller than other plants. Thus, genetic engineering enabled farmers to grow more fodder for cattle feed and larger, nicer ears of corn for the hundreds of things that utilize corn in their production. This effort to grow larger and healthier plants via the science of genetics began what was called the *green revolution,* which began in the 1940s. Through the work of Dr. Norman Borlaug, an American biologist, Mexico, for example, was able to develop a stronger wheat plant that produced twice as much grain. Prior to its development, hunger was a way of life for many in Mexico, because the country had to import half of its wheat, and many people could not afford to purchase the grain. With the development of the new strain of wheat, Mexico was able to supply its populace with affordable wheat and was even able to export wheat to other nations.

Much of the earth's populace lives on rice, including the people of India. In the early 1960s, India was on the brink of mass famine due to a rapidly growing population. Through the work of Dr. Borlaug and the Ford Foundation, a new variety of rice, called IR8, was developed. It was engineered to produce more grains per plant when grown with irrigation and fertilizers. Today, thanks to the green revolution, India is one of the world's leading producers of rice. Farmers in other parts of the world also began using IR8, and the development of hybrid plants went into full production. As a result, malnutrition in many countries was greatly reduced. The green revolution has alleviated food shortages in much of the world, except for parts of Africa, which have lagged behind due to internal problems.

In addition to discovering fertilizers and hybrids that resulted in faster and better yields, farmers also learned that they could now grow two crops per year on the same piece of land. This advance didn't come without a price, however, since fertilizing without allowing the land to rest resulted in each new crop being slightly less productive than the one before it. Monoculture farming, in which hundreds of acres of land are repeatedly planted with the same crop also began to exhaust the soil. China provides an example of what can happen when this type of farming is used. Since large portions of China's land have become unproductive, it is now transplanting entire communities to the unproductive land so the area the village once occupied can be utilized as farmland.[1] Salt from fertilizers have begun accumulating in the soil as well, making it unproductive. In fact, overfertilization, soil depletion, desertification, and deforestation of the world's soil has contributed to making eleven billion acres of land unproductive, which represents 45 percent of the earth's vegetated surface.

One of the main ingredients in fertilizer is

phosphate, and the African nations of Morocco and Western Sahara contains 80 percent of the world's supply. It is estimated that by 2030, the global demand for phosphate will exceed the supply. Global food production at that point will almost certainly plummet, meaning that ever-larger segments of the earth's population could suffer hunger. Burgeoning populations also require ever more land for housing; and as the earth's cities expand, a land area equivalent to the state of Maine is covered with concrete each year. One result is a growing implementation by city dwellers of urban agriculture in which people grow enough food to feed their own families on a small lot, or even in their backyards.

The demand for land and lumber is playing havoc with the world's rain forests. At one time, the rain forests covered 12 percent of the earth's surface; today, it is a mere 2 percent. One and a half acres of rain forest disappear every second, which equates to an area of land the size of New Jersey each year. The rain forests supply 20 percent of the earth's oxygen, and they recycle the carbon dioxide we produce. Yet, it is predicted that in twenty years the rain forests will be gone, along with the plants and species that inhabit them. In the interim, if immediate steps are not taken to stop the harvesting of lumber in the rain forests, the supply of the world's oxygen will decrease even more.

To summarize, we know that earth's population will continue to grow, resulting in corresponding increases in the demands for food and fertile land. We have reached our limit regarding land that is available for food and lumber production; in fact, each year we have less of it, not more. Making the fertile land we do have more productive will require more fertilizer, but as was previously mentioned, it is predicted that the supply of phosphate, a primary ingredient in fertilizer production, will be gone by 2030. These are not issues that can be postponed and addressed ten years down the road. They must be acted upon *now*. In fact, decades ago they were very serious issues that demanded humankind's immediate attention!

Land is not productive without water, and irrigation is another factor that has made it possible to grow larger and more plentiful crops. Many people are unaware that farming uses 70 percent of the world's fresh water supply. Industry uses 20 percent, and domestic use is 10 percent. As I write this book, water tables throughout the world continue to drop. Due to a prolonged drought, the state of California is searching for water by digging deeper wells. There are large bodies of fresh water underground called *aquifers.* The Ogallala Aquifer is located in the central United States. It is so large that it lies under parts of Nebraska, Colorado, Kansas, Oklahoma, New Mexico, and Texas. This area, called the "bread basket" of the world, produces a large amount of wheat, and the Ogallala Aquifer is the primary source of the water used to irrigate that wheat. At the present rate of use, the Ogallala Aquifer will be dry within the next twenty years!

Over one billion people worldwide are dependent upon glaciers for fresh water, but the glaciers are melting at an alarming rate. The average person in China uses eighty-six liters of fresh water a day, as China has had a fresh water shortage for years, while the average American uses five hundred liters a day. Unfortunately, water is not appreciated until the well runs dry.

Rainwater runs off the land into streams, which carry it into creeks, which run into rivers, which in turn flow into oceans. As the water runs off the land, it carries with it excess fertilizers and pesticides. Fertilizer causes algae to bloom, which is what the news is reporting when it calls our attention to a "red tide" in lakes or oceans. When these algal blooms occur, they suck most of the oxygen out of the water, which kills the fish and coral in that area and produces a "dead zone." Where the Mississippi River empties into the Gulf of Mexico, there is a dead zone covering sixty-seven hundred square miles in which no fish or coral can live. There are more than four hundred such dead zones throughout the world. Many scientists believe we have gone too far in depopulating the oceans, so that there is no way we can save them. British Petroleum (BP) spent more than forty billion dollars trying to clean up the mess it recently made in the Gulf of Mexico. But the dead zones are an even bigger problem than the BP oil spill.

As the years have passed and the earth's population has grown, the Wind of Natural Disasters has accelerated, and its force has become more destructive. Earth's natural resources are disappearing. Christ pointed to this as a sign of His return: "There will be signs in the sun, in the moon, and in the stars; and on the earth distress of nations, with perplexity, the sea and the waves roaring; men's hearts failing them from fear and the expectation of those things which are coming on the earth" (Luke 21:25, 26).

With each passing year, the problems grow larger and more perplexing. How will our divided world possibly unite to solve these crises? The situation doesn't look hopeful. But despite appearances, there really is cause for hope because the next verse states, "Then they will see the Son of Man coming in a cloud with power and great glory" (verse 27). Praise God! Jesus' soon return is the light at the end of earth's dark tunnel. "Now when these things begin to happen, look up and lift up your heads, because your redemption draws near" (verse 28).

1. Much of the information in this chapter is from chapter 4 of Scott Christiansen's book *Planet in Distress* (Hagerstown, MD: Review and Herald®, 2012), 38–52.

Chapter 2
The Wind of Change

Scripture speaks of a change of attitude in the last days: "And all the world marveled and followed the beast" (Revelation 13:3). Today, there is a wind blowing across the earth that is bringing about the fulfillment of this prophecy. In order to understand how this is happening, it is necessary to identify the beast mentioned in Revelation 13. Fortunately, Scripture gives us a number of identifying points so that we can know exactly who that beast is. The apostle John provides the following information about this prophetic symbol:

Then I stood on the sand of the sea. And I saw a beast rising up out of the sea, having seven heads and ten horns, and on his horns ten crowns, and on his heads a blasphemous name. Now the beast which I saw was like a leopard, his feet were like the feet of a bear, and his mouth like the mouth of a lion. The dragon gave him his power, his throne, and great authority. And I saw one of his heads as if it had been mortally wounded, and his deadly wound was healed. And all the world marveled and followed the beast. So they worshiped the dragon who gave authority to the beast; and they worshiped the beast, saying, "Who is like the beast? Who is able to make war with him?" And he was given a mouth speaking great things and blasphemies, and he was given authority to continue for forty-two months. Then he opened his mouth in blasphemy against God, to blaspheme His name, His tabernacle, and those who dwell in heaven. It was granted to him to make war with the saints and to overcome them. And authority was given him over every tribe, tongue, and nation. All who dwell on the earth will worship him, whose names have not been written in the Book of Life of the Lamb slain from the foundation of the world (verses 1–8).

Notice that this beast in Revelation 13 is composed of parts of three other beasts—a lion, a bear, and a leopard. Note also that the dragon gives him his power, his throne, and his great authority.

The prophetic books of Daniel and Revelation go together like a hand and glove. These four beasts—lion, bear, leopard, and dragon—are mentioned in the seventh chapter of Daniel. Scripture uses "beasts" (animals) in prophecy to represent nations, kingdoms, or powers. A study of Daniel 7 will show that the lion represents the ancient kingdom of Babylon; the bear represents the empire of Media-Persia; and the leopard represents the dominion of Greece. Chapter 12 of Revelation gives us the identity of the dragon, which we will find useful as we look at the rise and fall of nations.

Now a great sign appeared in heaven: a woman clothed with the sun, with the moon under her feet, and on her head a garland of twelve stars. Then being with child, she cried out in labor and in pain to give birth. And another sign appeared in heaven: behold, a great, fiery red dragon having seven heads and ten horns, and seven diadems on his heads. His tail drew a third of the stars of heaven and threw them to the earth. And the dragon stood before the woman who was ready to give birth, to devour her Child as soon as it was born. She bore a male Child who was to rule all nations with a rod of iron. And her Child was caught up to God and His throne. Then the woman fled into the wilderness, where she has a place prepared by God, that they should feed her there one thousand two hundred and sixty days (Revelation 12:1–6).

These verses contain a number of points that help us identify the various symbols referred to. The Bible identifies the dragon as the devil. We don't have to guess about this, because Revelation 12:9 makes it unmistakably clear: "So the great dragon was cast out, that serpent of old, called the Devil and Satan, who deceives the whole world; he was cast to the earth, and his angels were cast out with him." Verse 4 adds that "his tail drew a third of the stars of heaven and threw them to the earth." This is a reference to the one-third of the angels who followed Satan in rebellion against God and who were cast out of heaven with him.

We find that in Bible prophecy a woman represents a church or some type of religious power (Jeremiah 6:2; Isaiah 51:3). The woman in Revelation 12 symbolizes the pure, early Christian church. She is "clothed with the sun," which represents Christ, "the true Light which gives light to every man coming into the world" (John 1:9). The "moon under her feet" represents the Old Testament period, during which all the services and sacrifices of the sanctuary system were shadows—reflections—of things to come in the gospel of Jesus Christ, the Messiah.

Jesus is the only Person who meets the qualifications of the "male Child" that was born to the woman. "And the dragon stood before the woman who was ready to give birth, to devour her Child as soon as it was born. She bore a male Child who was to rule all nations with a rod of iron. And her Child was caught up to God and His throne" (Revelation 12:4, 5). The events surrounding the birth of Christ match this description precisely. The dragon (Satan) never operates openly; he always uses a person or a civil power to accomplish his purpose.

When the wise men were in search of the Christ child, their inquiry set Jerusalem in such an uproar that King Herod summoned them, asking who they were searching for. They told him they were seeking the child who was to be born a king. In response, Herod summoned the scribes, who told him the child was to be born in Bethlehem. Since Herod viewed the child as a rival to his throne, he sent the wise men away, telling them to inform him when they had found the child.

When the wise men didn't return, Herod used the civil power of Rome to slay all the male children in Bethlehem, two years of age and under (Matthew 2:1–18). Since a beast in prophecy represents a civil power, we can recognize that in this instance Satan (the primary dragon) is working through an agent (a secondary "dragon")—the civil power of the Roman Empire.

Returning now to our study of the beast brought to view in Revelation 13:1–8, we see the first clue to its identity. If the dragon (Satan, working through the civil power of the pagan Roman Empire) gives the beast "his power, his throne, and great authority" (verse 2), then the beast must appear on the scene of action *after* pagan Rome. What power arose following pagan Rome, receiving its power, authority, and throne from Rome?

History records that *pagan* Rome gave to *papal* Rome its throne and dominion. "Vigilius [the bishop of Rome], owing his pontificate to imperial influence, and bolstered by this new legal recognition of the pope's ecclesiastical supremacy, marked the beginning of a long climb toward political power."[1] Justinian, the emperor of Rome promised Vigilius a portion of temporal power. Now for the first time, the pope, the bishop of Rome, had civil power.

The next point of identification of this beast

is that "he was given authority to continue for forty-two months" (verse 5). One reason many people have difficulty understanding Bible prophecy is that they do not know the principles of interpretation given in Scripture itself. According to the Bible, in symbolic prophecies dealing with time, a *day* represents a literal *year*. God told the prophet Ezekiel, "I have laid on you a day for a year" (Ezekiel 4:6). The Bible also says, "According to the number of the days in which you spied out the land, forty days, for each day you shall bear your guilt one year, namely forty years" (Numbers 14:34). This understanding allows us to comprehend the prophecy, which states that the beast would have authority for forty-two months. Since there are thirty days in a biblical month, multiplying 30 days times 42 months equals 1,260 days. And since each day in symbolic prophecy equals a literal year, we know that this beast power would have authority for 1,260 literal years.

We learned in our previous point of identification that pagan Rome gave to papal Rome its authority and seat. This took place in A.D. 538.

The Wind of Change

"Vigilius . . . ascended the papal chair under the military protection of Belisarius [the general of the Roman army] (538–554)."[2] So papal Rome came into power in A.D. 538 and would be in authority for 1,260 years, which brings us to the year A.D. 1798. Let's go to our next clue to see what happened in 1798.

According to Bible prophecy, the beast would receive a deadly wound in 1798: "And I saw one of his heads as if it had been mortally wounded" (Revelation 13:3). It was at this time that Napoleon Bonaparte was attempting to unite Europe. Napoleon declared, "I wished to found a European system, a European code of laws, a European judiciary: there would be but one people in Europe."[3] Napoleon realized that he would be unable to accomplish his goal unless he overthrew the papal power. "In 1798 Berthier [Napoleon's general] made his entrance into Rome, abolished the papal government, and established a secular one."[4] After taking Pope Pius VI prisoner, General Berthier took him captive to France where he later died in exile. Prior to that time, the papacy owned large territories in central Italy known as the

Papal States, but these were all confiscated by Napoleon. When the papacy received its mortal wound, all the civil power that it had possessed for so many centuries was taken from it. This later became known as the Roman Question, which began in 1861 and was debated for the next sixty-eight years.

The Bible says that during the time of papal supremacy (538–1798), "it was granted to him to make war with the saints and to overcome them" (Revelation 13:7). This is the next point of identification of this beast power. During this 1,260-year period, millions of Christians were killed. For example, history records that during the Protestant Reformation (1517–1685) John Huss, Jerome of Prague, William Tyndale, and many other Reformers were strangled, burned at the stake, and slain with the sword. The Spanish Inquisition and the St. Bartholomew's Day Massacre are among a number of other well-known historical events in which thousands of Christians were persecuted and killed. "The Church of Rome has shed more innocent blood than any other institution that has ever existed among mankind."[5] When considering the amount of blood the Church of Rome has shed, please bear in mind the significant length of time involved—1,260 years.

Time has a way of making human tradition stronger than Scripture, which is what is involved in the next point of identification regarding the beast: "And he was given a mouth speaking great things and blasphemies" (Revelation 13:5). The biblical definition of *blasphemy* is a human claiming for himself or herself the prerogatives of God. For example, the Jewish leaders in Jesus' day accused Him of blasphemy when He said, "I and My Father are one" (John 10:30). They picked up stones to stone Him to death, and when Jesus asked them why, they replied, "For blasphemy, . . . because You, being a Man, make Yourself God" (verse 33).

On another occasion Jesus told a paralyzed man, "Your sins are forgiven you" (Luke 5:20). The scribes and Pharisees reasoned, "Who is this who speaks blasphemies? Who can forgive sins but God alone?" (verse 21). Of course, Christ did not commit blasphemy, because He truly *is* God. Consider, however, just two of the truly blasphemous statements made by the papal power: "We hold upon this earth the place of God Almighty."[6] "The priest does really and truly forgive the sin in virtue of the power given to him in Christ."[7]

The next clue to the identity of the beast involves the healing of a deadly wound that the beast received in 1798. The apostle John wrote, "I saw one of his heads as if it had been mortally wounded, and his deadly wound was healed" (Revelation 13:3). The "deadly wound" that the papacy received in 1798 began with what could be called the voluntary imprisonment of the popes. Stripped of their civil authority, the popes no longer had any influence in the affairs of the nations of the world. In protest, they retired into the Vatican and refused to appear in public. There were many efforts to settle the Roman Question, but the proposed solutions always depended on the Italian parliament, whose authority the papacy was unwilling to accept. As a result, negotiations between the Catholic Church and the Italian government continued for decades.

Finally, the Italian dictator Benito Mussolini

decided that he would settle the Roman Question, and on February 11, 1929, Italy signed the Lateran Treaty with the Vatican. It made the papacy a sovereign government with full rights to govern itself. Its agreed upon territory was Vatican City, and it was reimbursed 750,000,000 lira (approximately $21,000,000) for its loss of the Papal States. With the signing of this treaty, the Vatican was empowered to establish its own postal system and anything else necessary to organize and run a government. As a sovereign government, the Vatican was now able to send ambassadors to other nations and to receive ambassadors from them. In fact, if you wanted to find ambassadors from all over the world in a small area, you would go to Vatican City. Other than the Dalai Lama, the only religious leaders to have ever addressed the United Nations are the popes of Rome, because both are heads of sovereign nations. The "deadly wound" was healed—just as Scripture predicted.

This brings us to our last point in identifying this power: "And all the world marveled and followed the beast" (verse 3). Following 1798 and until the signing of the Lateran Treaty in 1929, the Roman Catholic Church was on the same level as all other churches. That is, it was a religious organization without any inherent *civil* or political power. However, following the healing of its "deadly wound," the Catholic Church has gone from being held in contempt by most nations to now being held in high esteem by much of the world. It has grown from a membership of approximately three hundred million in 1929 to over one *billion* members today. It has many ambassadors who have the ear of heads of state around the globe. Its counsel is sought on many major global decisions regarding not only religious and moral issues, but political ones as well. Most of this dramatic growth in its influence has occurred in recent years.

Pope John XXIII and Pope Paul VI laid the groundwork via the Second Vatican Council (1962–1965), which explored ways for the Catholic Church to reach out to other religious organizations. However, the Vatican's influence accelerated significantly with the election of Pope John Paul II, whose warm personality charmed the world. Traveling more than any other pope, he won the confidence and admiration of world leaders. For example, President Ronald Reagan sought his counsel in dealing with the problem of communism. Working together, they brought an end to the Soviet Union without a shot being fired. Many world leaders attended John Paul's funeral to show their respect, kneeling before his casket.

Today, a new pope—different than any other we have seen in modern times—has taken center stage. His humble, frugal life has won the hearts of people around the world. In just a few short years, Pope Francis has done much to change the negative press the Catholic Church had been receiving due to scandals involving child abuse and to place the church in a favorable position with the media. As a result, many members who had largely given up on the church are taking a second look.

These seven points of identification regarding the beast of Revelation 13:1–8 are so clear they are unmistakable. Taken in unison, they cannot apply to any other world power. According to Scripture, the papacy's influence will continue growing until almost the entire world will follow the beast. "And all the world marveled and followed the beast. . . . They worshiped the beast, saying, 'Who is like the beast?' " (verses 3, 4).

But this power, the papacy, is not the only power brought to view in Revelation 13. While the *first* beast of Revelation 13 was receiving its deadly wound, and while that deadly wound was healing, a *second* beast appeared. The apostle John saw it rising up out of the earth and growing powerful on the global scene of action. We will identify that second beast in the next chapter.

1. Le Roy Froom, *The Prophetic Faith of Our Fathers: The Historical Development of Prophetic Interpretation* (Washington, DC: Review and Herald®, 1950), 1:516.

2. Philip Schaff, *History of the Christian Church*, 3rd rev. ed. (New York: Charles Scribner, 1867), 2:327.

3. Robert Gibson, *Best of Enemies: Anglo-French Relations Since the Norman Conquest*, 2nd ed. (Exeter, UK: Impress Books, 2004), 157.

4. Alexander Hopkins McDannald, ed., *The Encyclopedia Americana* (Chicago: Americana Corporation, 1941).

5. W. E. H. Lecky, *History of the Rise and Influence of the Spirit of Rationalism in Europe*, 4th ed. (London:

Longmans, Green, and Co., 1870), 2:32.

6. Pope Leo XIII, *Praeclara Gratulationis Publicae* [The Reunion of Christendom], Papal Encyclicals.net, accessed June 15, 2015, http://www.papalencyclicals.net/Leo13/l13praec.htm.

7. Joseph Deharbe, *A Full Catechism of the Catholic Religion,* ed. P. N. Lynch, trans. John Fander (New York: Catholic School Book, 1876), 275.

Chapter 3
The Wind of Force

Then I saw another beast coming up out of the earth, and he had two horns like a lamb and spoke like a dragon. And he exercises all the authority of the first beast in his presence, and causes the earth and those who dwell in it to worship the first beast, whose deadly wound was healed. He performs great signs, so that he even makes fire come down from heaven on the earth in the sight of men. And he deceives those who dwell on the earth by those signs which he was granted to do in the sight of the beast, telling those who dwell on the earth to make an image to the beast who was wounded by the sword and lived. He was granted power to give breath to the image of the beast, that the image of the beast should both speak and cause as many as would not worship the image of the beast to be killed. He causes all, both small and great, rich and poor, free and slave, to receive a mark on their right hand or on their foreheads, and that no one may buy or sell except one who has the mark or the name of the beast, or the number of his name. Here is wisdom. Let him who has understanding calculate the number of the beast, for it is the number of a man: His number is 666 (Revelation 13:11–18).

Just as He did with the first beast of Revelation 13, God gives us identifying characteristics of this second, two-horned beast, brought to view in the chapter so that we might know the identity of the power it represents.

The first clue to help us identify this second beast involves the time period in which it arises. Speaking of the first beast power, the Bible says, "He who leads into captivity shall go into captivity, he who kills with the sword must be killed with the sword. Here is the patience and the faith of the saints" (verse 10). The papal power led thousands into captivity and had untold numbers killed with the sword. True to the prophecy, on February 10, 1798, the papacy received its deadly wound when Pope Pius VI was taken into captivity by Napoleon's general. Following his description of these events, the apostle John added, "Then I saw another beast coming up out of the earth" (verse 11). In other words, the second beast was rising as the first beast was falling. So the second beast arises in the time period of the late 1700s when the first beast is receiving its "deadly wound."

Verse 11 gives us another identifying characteristic of this second beast power. The first beast in Revelation 13 arose out of the sea (verse 1); the second beast came out of the earth (verse 11). In symbolic prophecy, water is used to represent a densely populated area: "The waters which you saw, where the harlot sits, are peoples, multitudes, nations, and tongues" (Revelation 17:15). So land or earth, being the opposite of water, would represent a sparsely populated area.

What new power arose in the 1700s in sparsely populated lands? The United States. America began, not with conquest, but with pilgrims who came seeking a new land where they could have freedom of worship and government. They arrived at Plymouth Rock in 1620 and began establishing villages. As the years passed, the population gradually grew until there were thirteen colonies that decided they wanted to be free of English rule and become an independent nation. In 1776, they wrote the Declaration of Independence and established their own government. The Bill of Rights was written in 1789 and passed in 1791. As we have already seen, the papacy was overthrown by Napoleon in 1798. Just as Scripture foretold, the beast from the sea, the papacy, was going into captivity during the same time period that the beast from the earth was rising. No nation other than the United States fits this time sequence. In 1754, John Wesley, a cofounder of the Methodist Church, wrote in reference to the second beast of Revelation 13: "He is not yet come, though he cannot be far off. For he is to appear at the end of the forty-two months of the first beast."[1]

Here is our next clue for identifying the second beast: "He had two horns like a lamb" (Revelation 13:11). As you study the beasts in Daniel and Revelation, you will find that some have seven horns, some have ten, and some have none. In Scripture, horns are used to represent power. If there is a crown on the horn, it means that the power would be ruled by a king or a monarch. If there are no crowns on the horns, as is the case with this two-horned beast in Revelation 13, it means that the power would be governed by the people. The United States was founded upon the twin principles of civil and religious liberty—a state without a monarch and a church without a pope. These two great principles have been the secret of its power and prosperity, and the conflict with England was fought over these two points of contention. Writing on the topic of liberty, particularly from British rule, in 1767, Josiah Quincy Jr. declared, "In defence of our civil and religious rights, . . . with the God of armies on our side, we fear not the hour of trial; tho' the host of our enemies should cover the field like locusts, . . . yet the sword of the Lord and of Gideon shall prevail."[2]

Revelation 13 goes on to compare this second beast to a lamb: "He had two horns like a lamb" (verse 11). This is the next point of identification. Comparing this beast to a lamb is extremely significant. Having "horns like a lamb" indicates that this is a new nation, not one that has existed for centuries. Even more significant is the fact that, in the Bible, Christ is represented as a Lamb. We are saved by "the precious blood of Christ, as of a lamb without blemish and without spot" (1 Peter 1:19). In heaven, angels around the throne exclaim, "Worthy is the Lamb who was slain to receive power and riches and wisdom" (Revelation 5:12).

America's founders were God-fearing, Bible-believing, Christian men and women, who used the Scriptures in determining how our nation would be governed. The first time I went to Washington, D.C., I was amazed at how many scriptural references are to be found throughout the city—on walls, plaques, and statues; in the Capitol; in the halls of Congress; and on various memorials.

Tragically however, the prophetic picture changes at this point. John wrote that, although the beast rising out of the earth appeared lamblike, it "spoke like a dragon" (Revelation 13:11). The Lamb is a symbol of Christ, so the dragon would be just the opposite—a symbol of the devil. In fact, as we have seen, the Bible clearly states that Satan is represented by the symbol of a dragon: "So the great dragon was cast out, that serpent of old, called the Devil and Satan, who deceives the whole world; he was cast to the earth, and his angels were cast out with him" (Revelation 12:9). Prophecy is clear; this nation—the United States, which was founded by people who served the Lord—will one day soon speak like Satan.

Next, Scripture goes on to describe what this second beast will do in partnership with the first beast of Revelation 13: "And he [the second beast] exercises all the authority of the first beast in his presence, and causes the earth and those who dwell in it to worship the first beast, whose deadly wound was healed" (verse 12).

Four Winds of Revelation

The prophecy does not picture the power and influence of the United States decreasing but increasing. During the time of papal supremacy (A.D. 538–1798), the beast from the sea (the Roman Catholic Church) had authority over many of the nations of Europe. One day soon, the beast from the earth—the United States—will exercise this same authority, not just over Europe, but over the entire world. Since papal Rome does not have armed forces of her own, she must turn to a civil power, the United States, to help enforce her decrees. The world was given a preview of this when Pope John Paul II worked with President Ronald Reagan to implement the overthrow of the Soviet Union.

America's founding fathers instituted a wall of separation between church and state to protect the state from the church, not to protect the church from the state. Although it has served the nation extremely well, that wall will crumble. Prophecy predicts that America will tell "those who dwell on the earth to make an image to the beast who was wounded by the sword and lived" (Revelation 13:14). An image is a replica or likeness of something else. Since the papacy has both religious *and* civil power, making an image or likeness of the first beast would mean that the second beast must also be a union of church and state.

"He [the second beast] was granted power to give breath to the image of the beast" (verse 15). To give breath to the image means to make it come alive; in other words, the United States will one day soon actively carry out the agenda of the papacy. The Bible states that the second beast "causes the earth and those who dwell in it to worship the first beast, whose deadly wound was healed" (verse 12). The word *causes* implies enforcement, indicating that the two-horned beast is a civil power; yet the element of worship is involved, signifying that it is also a religious power. Thus, like the Catholic Church, this second beast is a union of church and state.

The record is clear: never in the history of humankind has a church or religious organization, with access to civil power, been able to resist using the state's legislative and enforcement power to attempt to force its religious beliefs on others. Such attempts to evangelize by force occur because the religious organization believes its doctrines are true and correct and that everyone should accept them regardless of the circumstances. Typically, as in the case of Christians afflicting "heretics" in the past or in the case of Muslims persecuting Christians today, the tormentors justify their religious persecution of others with the belief that they are "saving" those whom they persecute.

Our religious beliefs cannot be based on the doctrines of any religious denomination or group because hundreds if not thousands exist, and they all believe they are right. Our only safety is in the Word of God. It is vital that we know what the Bible teaches, so that we can walk as God leads us (Psalm 119:105). Only when our beliefs agree with Scripture can we be assured of not being deceived and of standing on solid ground.

Consider what the two-horned beast, the United States, will soon do: "He causes all, both small and great, rich and poor, free and slave, to receive a mark on their right hand or on their foreheads" (Revelation 13:16). Having the mark "on their foreheads" refers to those who worship the beast because they agree with its teachings, with what it is enforcing. Having the mark "on their right hand" represents those who cooperate, who go along with what is being enforced in order to avoid being persecuted, even though they may not agree with it. It is easy to say one believes something when it requires no sacrifice or in order to avoid persecution, but God is looking for men and women who are willing to stand upon His Word by faith and to remain true to Him regardless of the consequences. When God's final end-time test comes upon humankind, only those who through faith in Jesus Christ and in the Bible's teachings, only those whose faith endures to the end, will receive salvation: Jesus says, "Yes, the time is coming that whoever kills you will think that he offers God service" (John 16:2). "Be faithful until death, and I will give you the crown of life" (Revelation 2:10).

Tragically, the support given by the second beast (the United States) to the first beast (the Roman Catholic Church) will enforce the mark of the first beast, a mark that the great majority of humankind will receive (Revelation 13:3,

4). Revelation 13:17, 18 refers to the number 666, helping to identify the first beast, stating that "it is the number of a man" and "the number of his name." Since we have identified the first beast as the Roman Catholic Church, this reference is clearly to the pope, the man at its head.

In the next chapter, we will see how all of this will take place. God's angels have been holding the winds of strife back from blowing, but they are now beginning to be released. God is moving to rapidly bring about the conditions necessary to accomplish all the things His Word states will occur at the end time, the time in which we live.

1. John Wesley, *Explanatory Notes Upon the New Testament,* 4th American ed. (New York: J. Soule and T. Mason, 1818), 735.

2. Josiah Quincy Jr. [Hyperion, pseud.], *Boston Gazette, and Country Journal,* October 5, 1767, accessed July 9, 2015, http://www.masshist.org/dorr/volume/1/sequence /735.

Chapter 4
The Wind of Compromise

How will the beast with two horns cause all people on earth to receive marks on their foreheads or on their right hands? To answer this question, we need to go to the seventeenth chapter of Revelation, where we find a scarlet colored beast:

Then one of the seven angels who had the seven bowls came and talked with me, saying to me, "Come, I will show you the judgment of the great harlot who sits on many waters, with whom the kings of the earth committed fornication, and the inhabitants of the earth were made drunk with the wine of her fornication."

So he carried me away in the Spirit into the wilderness. And I saw a woman sitting on a scarlet beast which was full of names of blasphemy, having seven heads and ten horns. The woman was arrayed in purple and scarlet, and adorned with gold and precious stones and pearls, having in her hand a golden cup full of abominations and the filthiness of her fornication. And on her forehead a name was written:

MYSTERY, BABYLON THE GREAT,
THE MOTHER OF HARLOTS
AND OF THE ABOMINATIONS
OF THE EARTH.

I saw the woman, drunk with the blood of the saints and with the blood of the martyrs of Jesus. And when I saw her, I marveled with great amazement (Revelation 17:1–6).

Before continuing to examine the rest of chapter 17, let's pause and consider what these first six verses have stated. You will recall that in Bible prophecy, a beast symbolizes a nation, kingdom, or some type of civil power. However, here we find a woman sitting on a beast. In prophecy, a woman represents a church: " 'For this reason a man shall leave his father and mother and be joined to his wife, and the two shall become one flesh.' This is a great mystery, but I speak concerning Christ and the church" (Ephesians 5:31, 32). Revelation 12 presents a pure woman, whereas Revelation 17 brings to view an impure woman. Her act of riding the beast represents that she is in control of it. The text also states that she "sits on many waters" (Revelation 17:1). Since water in Bible prophecy stands for multitudes of peoples (see verse 15), this indicates that multitudes of people are under this woman's jurisdiction. Clearly, this passage is referring to a large church with a large membership, so much so that "the inhabitants of the earth were made drunk with the wine of her fornication" (verse 2). The "wine of her fornication" represents her false teachings that multitudes have embraced and followed. These people are represented as being "drunk," because they are under the influence of her wine, and it is difficult to reason with drunk people.

Revelation 17:2 also states that "the kings of the earth committed fornication" with this woman/church, meaning that she is a combination of religious *and* political power. Committing fornication means that she is in bed with the kings, the secular powers, of the earth. This is certainly true today, since the papacy has ambassadors in 106 countries of the world. No major international decisions are made without consulting her.

Revelation 17:6 provides yet another point of identification regarding this woman called "Babylon": "I saw the woman, drunk with the blood of the saints and with the blood of the martyrs of Jesus." History is full of the accounts of persecution carried out by the Roman Catholic Church during the Dark Ages, including the persecution of Dutch Protestants, the Spanish Inquisition, and the St. Bartholomew's Day Massacre.

The Roman Catholic Church is the only church that fits all of these characteristics. Millions of people within the Catholic Church are sincere Christians that God numbers among His people. That is why God is calling to them, "Come out of her, my people, lest you share in her sins, and lest you receive of her plagues" (Revelation 18:4).

Now, let's unravel the remainder of Revelation 17. These verses will help us understand what is happening today and what we can look for in the future.

> But the angel said to me, "Why did you marvel? I will tell you the mystery of the woman and of the beast that carries her, which has the seven heads and the ten horns. The beast that you saw was, and is not, and will ascend out of the bottomless pit and go to perdition. And those who dwell on the earth will marvel, whose names are not written in the Book of Life from the foundation of the world, when they see the beast that was, and is not, and yet is.
>
> "Here is the mind which has wisdom: The seven heads are seven mountains on which the woman sits. There are also

seven kings. Five have fallen, one is, and the other has not yet come. And when he comes, he must continue a short time. The beast that was, and is not, is himself also the eighth, and is of the seven, and is going to perdition.

"The ten horns which you saw are ten kings who have received no kingdom as yet, but they receive authority for one hour as kings with the beast. These are of one mind, and they will give their power and authority to the beast. These will make war with the Lamb, and the Lamb will overcome them, for He is Lord of lords and King of kings; and those who are with Him are called, chosen, and faithful."

Then he said to me, "The waters which you saw, where the harlot sits, are peoples, multitudes, nations, and tongues. And the ten horns which you saw on the beast, these will hate the harlot, make her desolate and naked, eat her flesh and burn her with fire. For God has put it into their hearts to fulfill His purpose, to be of one mind, and to give their kingdom to the beast, until the words of God are fulfilled. And the woman whom you saw is that great city which reigns over the kings of the earth" (verses 7–18).

Please notice that in Revelation 17:7, God makes a clear distinction between the woman and the beast: "I will tell you the mystery of the woman and of the beast that carries her, which has the seven heads and the ten horns." This distinction becomes necessary as we proceed further in understanding this chapter.

As previously mentioned, in prophecy a woman represents a church or religious organization, and a beast represents a civil power. Since a church has no inherent civil power, she must rely upon a civil government to enforce her rules or doctrines. The fact that the woman is riding the beast symbolizes that the church is in control of the civil government.

The Lord does not want anyone to be in doubt regarding the identity of this beast, so He gives us a puzzle to solve that will enable us to identify it: "Here is the mind which has wisdom: The seven heads are seven mountains on which the woman sits. There are also seven kings. Five have fallen, one is, and the other has not yet come. And when he comes, he must continue a short time. The beast that was, and is not, is himself also the eighth, and is of the seven, and is going to perdition" (verses 9–11).

We dare not add our own interpretation to the prophecy (2 Peter 1:20); instead, we need only read other prophetic books in the Bible that mention "beasts." The clearest representation of beasts as nations is found in the book of Daniel—in the second and seventh chapters. There we find four beasts that cover the period of time from 605 B.C. until A.D. 1798. They are as follows:

The lion represents Babylon (Daniel 7:4).
The bear represents Media-Persia (Daniel 7:5).
The leopard represents Greece (Daniel 7:6).
The dragonlike beast represents pagan Rome (Daniel 7:7).

The Roman Empire can be divided into two time periods: pagan Rome (168 B.C.–A.D. 476), and papal Rome (A.D. 538–A.D. 1798). Out of the dragon (pagan Rome) came a little horn power, which is papal Rome (Daniel 7:20). Revelation 13 picks up where Daniel 7 leaves off. Revelation 13:1 presents the papacy as "a beast rising up out of the sea."

We can now return to the prophecy in Revelation 17, which states, "Five [kings] have fallen" (verse 10). History records that the prophecy was fulfilled exactly as Scripture predicted: Babylon fell to Media-Persia in 539 B.C.; the Persian Empire fell to Greece in 331 B.C.; the Grecian kingdom fell to pagan Rome in 168 B.C.; the pagan Roman Empire was succeeded by papal Rome in A.D. 538; and the papacy fell to the atheistic power of France in A.D. 1798. These are the five kings that have fallen.

This began what John refers to in Revelation 17:3 as the "wilderness," where he saw the "scarlet beast." Of the "seven heads" on the beast, he says, "There are also seven kings. Five have fallen, one is, and the other has not yet come. And when he comes, he must continue a short time" (verse 10). Bear in mind that John is in vision in the wilderness and that we must look at this prophecy from his point of view. When he says that "one [king] is" (present tense), John is speaking from the perspective of the time of the "wilderness," following the fall of the fifth king, papal Rome, in 1798, when Napoleon's General Berthier marched into Rome; took Pope Pius VI prisoner; and set up a secular, atheistic government.

Due to ignorance and the abuse of power, that era was rife with rebellion against governments and religion. Through the writings of Thomas Paine and others, deism, leading to atheism, was spreading across Europe and the United States. France led the way with the Age of Reason, out of which was born the ideas that produced the godless society that John saw as a "wilderness." From these ideas came Darwin's theory of evolution and Karl Marx's ideas, which led to atheistic communism. Both of these theories attacked the faith of millions, and Marx's theory took on civil power. Therefore, Marxism seems to be presented in Scripture as the sixth beast.

During this period, God did not stand idly by. In order to put His Word into as many hands as possible and to meet the spread of Darwinism and atheism, the British Bible Society and the American Bible Society were born.

Meanwhile, across the sea, the seventh beast with "two horns like a lamb" (Revelation 13:11) was slowly rising out of the earth. From the perspective of the "wilderness," John could say he "has not yet come" (Revelation 17:10). The United States was just in the process of putting together a government. It was God's will that this should be a Christian nation, which would be a bulwark against the rise of atheism. It is presented in Scripture as having "two horns like a lamb," because it was to be Christlike in character.

Now for the final clue: "The beast that was, and is not, is himself also the eighth, and is of the seven, and is going to perdition" (verse 11). Significantly, the Bible states very clearly that this eighth beast is one "of the seven." This eighth beast that the woman is riding has to be a beast that "was" (in the past), and "is not" (in the present), and "yet is" (in the future). When we consider this statement from John's point of view in the wilderness, only one of the seven beasts fits this description. The papacy was in existence as both a civil and religious power from A.D. 538 until A.D. 1798, when it was stripped of its civil power by Napoleon. As we have seen earlier, the papacy did not regain its civil power until the Lateran Treaty was signed in 1929. Since in Bible prophecy a beast represents a civil power, the papacy was "not" from 1798 until 1929, yet today it "is" again a civil power, as well as a religious one. Since God is the same yesterday, today, and forever, He does not change; therefore, the Bible, which is His inspired Word, does not change.

The "ten kings" (verse 12) are the same as those found in Daniel 7; they represent the nations of modern Europe. "These are of one mind, and they will give their power and authority to the beast" (Revelation 17:13). It is interesting to note that the two-horned beast of Revelation 13, the United States, will also give homage to this beast "telling those who dwell on the earth to make an image to the beast who was wounded by the sword and lived" (verse 14). Clearly, there will be something in common, some unifying point of agreement, between the nations of Europe, the United States, and the papacy.

The Wind of Compromise

Revelation 16:13, 14 provides an interesting insight: "And I saw three unclean spirits like frogs coming out of the mouth of the dragon, out of the mouth of the beast, and out of the mouth of the false prophet. For they are spirits of demons, performing signs, which go out to the kings of the earth and of the whole world, to gather them to the battle of that great day of God Almighty." We have seen so far that the dragon represents pagan Rome and that the beast symbolizes the papacy. But who is the "false prophet"? Revelation 19:20 states, "Then the beast was captured, and with him the false prophet who worked signs in his presence, by which he deceived those who received the mark of the beast and those who worshiped his image." This text states that the false prophet is one who works signs (miracles) and deceives those who receive the beast's mark. This is exactly what Revelation 13 states regarding the work of the two-horned beast, the United States.

What do the dragon, the beast, and the false prophet have in common? They each have "unclean spirits like frogs" coming out of their mouths. And how do frogs catch their prey? With their tongues. These false prophets seek to deceive others via their spiritual beliefs. The dragon's belief is paganism; the beast's is Roman Catholicism; and the false prophet's is apostate Protestantism. Therefore, whatever the three unite on, it must be something on which paganism, Catholicism, and Protestantism all agree.

One unbiblical belief they hold in common is the doctrine of the immortality of the soul. This idea found its way into the church through Greek philosophy, for the Greeks believed that the soul cannot die and that it is set free when a person dies.

To understand what the Bible teaches on this subject, let's begin with Scripture's definition of a soul: "And the LORD God formed man of the dust of the ground, and breathed into his nostrils the breath of life; and man became a living being ["soul," KJV]" (Genesis 2:7). The text does not state that God combined man's body, the breath of life, and the soul; it states that He combined the body and the breath of life, and that this combination of the two "became [formed] a living being" or "soul." A body plus God's breath of life are required to form a soul. In other words, you do not *possess* a soul, you *are* a soul.

In my opinion, there are two texts that settle this question. The first states that God alone possesses immortality today. "He [God] who is the blessed and only Potentate, the King of kings and Lord of lords, who alone has immortality" (1 Timothy 6:15, 16). And the second text declares that God will bestow immortality as a gift to the redeemed at their resurrection when Jesus comes.

> Behold, I tell you a mystery: We shall not all sleep, but we shall all be changed—in a moment, in the twinkling of an eye, at the last trumpet. For the trumpet will sound, and the dead will be raised incorruptible, and we shall be changed. For this corruptible must put on incorruption, and this mortal must put on immortality. So when this corruptible has put on incorruption, and this mortal has put on immortality, then shall be brought to pass the saying

that is written: "Death is swallowed up in victory" (1 Corinthians 15:51–54).

Can a "soul" die? The Bible answers Yes. Jesus Himself said, "And do not fear those who kill the body but cannot kill the soul. But rather fear Him who is able to destroy both soul and body in hell" (Matthew 10:28). "The soul of the father as well as the soul of the son is Mine; the soul who sins shall die" (Ezekiel 18:4). We were created by the hand of God; therefore, He can give life or take it away.

The Bible refers to death as a sleep. "Behold, I tell you a mystery: We shall not all sleep, but we shall all be changed" (1 Corinthians 15:51). In speaking to His disciples about the death of Lazarus, Jesus said, "Our friend Lazarus sleeps, but I go that I may wake him up" (John 11:11). Christ possesses the power to speak and bring the dead to life: "Do not marvel at this; for the hour is coming in which all who are in the graves will hear His voice" (John 5:28). It is at the resurrection of the redeemed that the saved will receive immortality—and not until then.

Another unbiblical doctrine that paganism,

The Wind of Compromise

Catholicism, and apostate Protestantism hold in common is the doctrine of the eternal torment of the wicked. This unscriptural idea also originated in Greek philosophy and is closely related to the idea that the soul is immortal. The Greeks believed that the body was the prison house of the soul and that when a person died the soul was set free and went to heaven or hell. They believed a Greek god named Hades ruled over the underworld. In time, "Hades" came to be applied to the underworld, or hell, as well as being the name of the god who ruled there. The Greek philosophers Socrates and Plato gave impetus to this idea, particularly in the description of Socrates's death.

The word *Hades* or *hell* is not used in the Old Testament; however, the Old Testament does speak of the total destruction of the wicked:

"For behold, the day is coming,
Burning like an oven,
And all the proud, yes, all who do wickedly
    will be stubble.
And the day which is coming shall burn
    them up,"

Says the LORD of hosts,
"That will leave them neither root nor
    branch.
But to you who fear My name
The Sun of Righteousness shall arise
With healing in His wings;
And you shall go out
And grow fat like stall-fed calves.
You shall trample the wicked,
For they shall be ashes under the soles of
    your feet
On the day that I do this,"
Says the LORD of hosts (Malachi 4:1–3).

The Flood, described in Genesis, teaches what
will happen to the wicked. The Bible says, "And
all flesh died that moved on the earth: birds
and cattle and beasts and every creeping thing
that creeps on the earth, and every man. . . .
So He [God] destroyed all living things which
were on the face of the ground: both man and
cattle, creeping thing and bird of the air. They
were destroyed from the earth" (Genesis 7:21,
23). When Scripture states that all flesh "died,"
it does not mean that individuals continued

living. Death is the cessation of life, not the continuation of it. And the New Testament specifically uses the Flood to illustrate the fate of the wicked. "For this they [the wicked] willfully forget: that by the word of God the heavens were of old, and the earth standing out of water and in the water, by which the world that then existed perished, being flooded with water. But the heavens and the earth which are now preserved by the same word, are reserved for fire until the day of judgment and perdition of ungodly men" (2 Peter 3:5–7). The word *perished* means to cease to exist, and Peter applies it to the end of time when "ungodly men" will be destroyed by fire just as they were once destroyed by water in the Flood.

As an example of the complete destruction of the wicked, Scripture refers us to what happened to Sodom and Gomorrah when "the LORD rained brimstone and fire on Sodom and Gomorrah, from the LORD out of the heavens" (Genesis 19:24). To emphasize the point, Peter again describes how completely the fire did its work. He says that God turned "the cities of Sodom and Gomorrah into ashes," and "condemned them to destruction, making them an example to those who afterward would live ungodly" (2 Peter 2:6). Clearly, the ungodly will be completely and eternally destroyed by being burned to "ashes." Jude refers to the same thing in Jude 7: "Sodom and Gomorrah, and the cities around them in a similar manner to these, having given themselves over to sexual immorality and gone after strange flesh, are set forth as an example, suffering the vengeance of eternal fire." This is what the "second death," the eternal death of the wicked, will be like when God executes judgment (see Revelation 2:11; 20:6, 14; 21:8). "Eternal fire" does not mean that the fire will never go out; rather, it means that the *results* of the fire will be eternal. Sodom and Gomorrah are not burning today; once the fire reduced these cities to ashes, it went out. But the result of that fire—total destruction—was everlasting.

The misunderstanding of a word can cause much confusion. Matthew 25:46 states, "And these [the wicked] will go away into everlasting punishment, but the righteous into eternal life." Many have understood this text to say that the wicked will suffer forever. However, the text speaks of everlasting *punishment,* not everlasting *punishing.* There is a big difference. Once the wicked are burned to ashes, they will be gone—just as though they had never existed or been created (Obadiah 16; Psalm 9:5, 6; 37:10, 20, 36). That is the punishment, and it will be everlasting. Never will the wicked exist again. But they will not be burning forever.

Other words from Jesus also emphasize the Bible teaching that the wicked will be completely done away with. Jesus said, "Do not fear those who kill the body but cannot kill the soul. But rather fear Him who is able to destroy both soul and body in hell" (Matthew 10:28). The word here translated as "hell" is the Greek word *Gehenna,* which referred to a place outside Jerusalem called the Valley of Hinnom. It was the city dump, where trash and dead (not live) animals were brought to be burned and where the fire consumed whatever the worms (maggots) did not. In Mark 9:47, 48, Christ describes this as a place of total destruction: "And if your eye causes you to sin, pluck it out. It is better for you to enter the kingdom of God with one eye, rather than having two eyes, to be cast into hell fire—where 'Their worm does not die and the fire is not quenched.' "

The Bible teaches that hell is a place where all signs of sinners and sin will be eliminated. "The day of the Lord will come as a thief in the night, in which the heavens will pass away with a great noise, and the elements will melt with fervent heat; both the earth and the works that are in it will be burned up. . . . Nevertheless we, according to His promise, look for new heavens and a new earth in which righteousness dwells" (2 Peter 3:10, 13).

The dragon, the beast, and the false prophet are all in agreement regarding this great deception that the wicked are tormented eternally in hellfire. It is taught by paganism, Catholicism, and Protestantism, but it has no foundation whatsoever in Scripture. Once God's judgment is completed, sinners and all the signs of sin will be eternally gone; and righteousness will reign. This is clearly *not* the eternal-burning teaching of paganism that was brought into the Catholic Church and subsequently passed on to her daughters, the Protestant churches—a doctrine that all three accept. There are many other things they hold in common, but let's consider one more.

If we go back in history as far as the tower of Babel, we find that paganism existed even then. Scripture states, "Cush begot Nimrod; he began to be a mighty one on the earth. He was a mighty hunter before the LORD; therefore it is said, 'Like Nimrod the mighty hunter before the LORD.' And the beginning of his kingdom was Babel, Erech, Accad, and Calneh, in the land of Shinar" (Genesis 10:8–10). One of the cities Nimrod built was Babel (known to us as Babylon), which became one of the major cities of the ancient world. According to the book *The Two Babylons,* by Alexander Hislop, Nimrod was killed after becoming king, and his wife, Semiramis, took over the throne. She told the people that her husband had gone to the sun and that he was now the god of the sun. Nimrod became known under different names such as Baal or Merodach. Just as the sun advances from east to west, never turning back, so Nimrod was considered to be a god of conquest who always went forward, never backward. Semiramis became pregnant and told the people she had conceived by her spirit husband, the sun. They worshiped her as a goddess of fertility; and when she gave birth, they deified her son, whom she named Tammuz. The people believed that Tammuz died every fall and was resurrected every spring.

In New Testament times, Semiramis was known by the name Diana. This pagan goddess is mentioned in an account of Paul's experience in Ephesus when a riot broke out. "When the city clerk had quieted the crowd, he said: 'Men of Ephesus, what man is there who does not know that the city of the Ephesians is temple guardian of the great goddess Diana, and of the image which fell down from Zeus?' " (Acts 19:35).

We find an example of God's people worshiping these pagan gods in Ezekiel 8:13–16. The prophet says,

> And He said to me, "Turn again, and you will see greater abominations that they are doing." So He brought me to the door of the north gate of the LORD's house; and

to my dismay, women were sitting there weeping for Tammuz.

Then He said to me, "Have you seen this, O son of man? Turn again, you will see greater abominations than these." So He brought me into the inner court of the Lord's house; and there, at the door of the temple of the Lord, between the porch and the altar, were about twenty-five men with their backs toward the temple of the Lord and their faces toward the east, and they were worshiping the sun toward the east.

This pagan worship stood in direct contrast to what the Bible teaches. God gave humanity a commandment, which if His people had followed it, would have stopped the worship of pagan gods and minimized the influence of paganism. They would have worshiped the Lord, the Creator of heaven and earth, instead of the gods of paganism. That commandment is the fourth commandment of the Decalogue, which reads:

"Remember the Sabbath day, to keep it holy. Six days you shall labor and do all your work, but the seventh day is the Sabbath of the LORD your God. In it you shall do no work: you, nor your son, nor your daughter, nor your male servant, nor your female servant, nor your cattle, nor your stranger who is within your gates. For in six days the LORD made the heavens and the earth, the sea, and all that is in them, and rested the seventh day. Therefore the LORD blessed the Sabbath day and hallowed it" (Exodus 20:8–11).

God established the seventh day of the week as the Sabbath—a day for His people to worship Him as the Creator of heaven and earth. This fourth commandment would have kept humankind aware of the fact that there is no other God. The Creator blessed and hallowed the seventh day, making it a day that belonged to Him: "Six days you shall labor and do all your work, but the seventh day is the Sabbath of the LORD your God" (verses 9, 10).

Under paganism's influence, the church

changed the day of worship from the seventh day to the first day of the week. This was a result of pagan sun worship, which is why the first day of the week is named Sunday. There are no texts in the Bible that state we should worship God on the first day of the week. In fact, there are only eight texts in the Bible that even mention the first day of the week. Let's look at each of these.

The first is Genesis 1:5: "God called the light Day, and the darkness He called Night. So the evening and the morning were the first day." There is nothing in this text about the first day being a day of worship. In fact, it is Genesis that says God blessed the seventh day of the week and sanctified it (set it apart for holy use). "On the seventh day God ended His work which He had done, and He rested on the seventh day from all His work which He had done. Then God blessed the seventh day and sanctified it, because in it He rested from all His work which God had created and made" (Genesis 2:2, 3).

The next four texts that mention the first day of the week—Matthew 28:1; Mark 16:2; Luke 24:1; John 20:1—are in the New Testament and refer to Christ's resurrection on the first day of the week. Nothing in these four texts states that Christ set the first day aside as a day of worship. In fact, the opposite is true: "The women who had come with Him [Jesus] from Galilee followed after, and they observed the tomb and how His body was laid. Then they returned and prepared spices and fragrant oils. And they rested on the Sabbath according to the commandment" (Luke 23:55, 56). These women knew nothing about a change in the day of worship, yet they were some of Jesus' closest followers. In fact, concerning Jesus' resurrection, Matthew states that it occurred on the first day of the week, "after the Sabbath . . ." (Matthew 28:1).

The sixth text appears in John's Gospel. He speaks of Jesus appearing to His disciples that evening following His resurrection. "Then, the same day at evening, being the first day of the week, when the doors were shut where the disciples were assembled, for fear of the Jews, Jesus came and stood in the midst, and said to them, 'Peace be with you' " (John 20:19). It is very clear that the disciples were not there worshiping but hiding. They were afraid that they would be arrested for following Christ. They were still unsure whether Jesus had risen and what was going to happen to them. Once again, we find nothing in this text about any change of the day of worship.

The Bible contains only two more texts that mention the first day of the week. The first of these is Acts 20:7–11:

> Now on the first day of the week, when the disciples came together to break bread, Paul, ready to depart the next day, spoke to them and continued his message until midnight. There were many lamps in the upper room where they were gathered together. And in a window sat a certain young man named Eutychus, who was sinking into a deep sleep. He was overcome by sleep; and as Paul continued speaking, he fell down from the third story and was taken up dead. But Paul went down, fell on him, and embracing him said, "Do not trouble yourselves, for his life is in him." Now when he had come up, had broken

bread and eaten, and talked a long while, even till daybreak, he departed.

Some have said that this text describes a preaching service on the first day of the week and, therefore, is evidence that the apostle Paul considered Sunday to be the new day of worship. So let's look at this text carefully; it contains a number of points that we need to consider.

This was an evening meeting on the first day of the week; in fact, it lasted all that night until daybreak. We need to remember the biblical way of reckoning time. Throughout the Scriptures, time is reckoned from evening until evening; the day begins at sundown and ends the following sundown. At creation, "God called the light Day, and the darkness He called Night. So the evening and the morning were the first day" (Genesis 1:5). Later, God instructed, "From evening to evening, you shall celebrate your sabbath" (Leviticus 23:32). In biblical time reckoning, then, the first day of the week begins at sunset on Sabbath (Saturday) evening. This means that this meeting in Acts took place on Saturday night. The text states that Paul departed the next day, which meant that he left in the daylight hours on Sunday morning and walked nineteen miles to Assos to catch a ship (Acts 20:13, 14). Again, we find nothing here about the first day being a special day of worship; on the contrary, it was no different than our going to a prayer meeting on Wednesday night.

The final Bible text that mentions the first day of the week is 1 Corinthians 16:1, 2. "Now concerning the collection for the saints, as I have given orders to the churches of Galatia, so you must do also: On the first day of the week let each one of you lay something aside, storing up as he may prosper, that there be no collections when I come." This was Paul's instruction to the churches at Corinth and Galatia regarding an offering for the poor in Jerusalem. Again, some have said that this verse refers to taking up an offering in church on the first day of the week, indicating that the worship day had been changed to Sunday.

But the text says nothing of a church service. Paul tells the people to "lay something aside," meaning to do so at home, not at church. This is what the Greek words imply. Paul was telling them that on the first day of each week they should consider how God had blessed them, and then set aside an appropriate amount for the poor ("lay something aside, storing up as he may prosper") so their offering would be accumulated and ready when he returned.

Another reason Paul stressed "that there be no collections when I come" is that charitable giving then was not as simple as it is today. Very few people had coinage; most exchange was done via the bartering system. For example, a person could take a bushel of wheat to the market and trade it for two bushels of barley, etc. So it took some planning to have an offering ready for Paul to take with him when he arrived.

Does this text state that the first day of the week is a day of worship or a holy day? No. Does it command God's people to gather on the first day of the week for a church service? No. Does it state that they were meeting each first day for worship? No. Does it refer to a public meeting? No. There is nothing in this passage that makes Sunday a special day of worship. Instead, the Bible consistently teaches that the seventh day of the week (Saturday) is the Sabbath, the day God set aside as the weekly day of worship. There is no question that God's people kept the Sabbath throughout Old and New Testament times; in fact, there is not one follower of God in the entire Bible who was not a Sabbath keeper.

The Scriptures are unmistakably clear that Jesus kept the Sabbath (Mark 2:27, 28; Luke 4:16), and since the twelve disciples were followers of Jesus, we can safely conclude that they kept the Sabbath as well. There is not one incident in the Bible where they did anything other than that.

Now, let's consider a person who did not have the privilege of walking and talking with Jesus while He was here on earth—the apostle Paul. In explaining his experience on the road to Damascus, Paul stated, "Then last of all He [Jesus] was seen by me also, as by one born out of due time" (1 Corinthians 15:8). Since Paul became the apostle to the Gentiles, let's consider how he related the question of the Sabbath to the Gentiles.

The Bible tells us that in Antioch, after Paul

had finished preaching in the synagogue to the Jews, "when the Jews went out of the synagogue, the Gentiles begged that these words might be preached to them the next Sabbath. Now when the congregation had broken up, many of the Jews and devout proselytes followed Paul and Barnabas, who, speaking to them, persuaded them to continue in the grace of God. On the next Sabbath almost the whole city came together to hear the word of God" (Acts 13:42–44). Don't miss this essential point: the Gentiles begged Paul to preach to them "the next Sabbath," which he did when almost the entire city, Jews *and* Gentiles, came together to hear God's Word. If the Sabbath had been changed to the first day of the week, this was the perfect opportunity for Paul to tell the people about the change—yet he did no such thing. He didn't tell the Gentiles, "Oh, you don't have to wait until the next Sabbath. The first day of the week is the new, Christian day of worship, so we'll meet tomorrow." Why didn't he? Because Christ had instituted no such change—not before His death and resurrection nor after it.

The Wind of Compromise

Paul once had a vision in which a man in Macedonia asked him to go there and help them. The event is recorded in Acts 16:10–13:

> Now after he [Paul] had seen the vision, immediately we sought to go to Macedonia, concluding that the Lord had called us to preach the gospel to them. Therefore, sailing from Troas, we ran a straight course to Samothrace, and the next day came to Neapolis, and from there to Philippi, which is the foremost city of that part of Macedonia, a colony. And we were staying in that city for some days. And on the Sabbath day we went out of the city to the riverside, where prayer was customarily made; and we sat down and spoke to the women who met there.

At this time in history, few Jews had migrated into Macedonia, so there was no synagogue in the city of Philippi. However, when the Sabbath arrived, Paul's group found a place where a few people were meeting by the riverside. Keeping the Sabbath was not something that Paul did occasionally. "And he reasoned in the synagogue [at Corinth] every Sabbath, and persuaded both Jews and Greeks" (Acts 18:4).

We have found in the Bible that Jesus, the apostles, the Jews, and the Gentile believers all kept the Sabbath. There is no scriptural foundation for any weekly day of worship other than the seventh-day Sabbath. God gave humans six days in which to labor and do all their work (Exodus 20:9), but the seventh day, the Sabbath, belongs to Him. The Bible says, "The seventh day is the Sabbath of the LORD your God" (verse 10). He commands us to "remember the Sabbath day, to keep it holy" (verse 8).

What do the dragon (paganism), the beast (Catholicism), and the false prophet (apostate Protestantism) hold in common? They share the following three beliefs: the immortality of the soul, the eternal torment of the wicked, and Sunday as the weekly day of worship. These three beliefs all come from human tradition (Matthew 15:1–9) and have no foundation whatsoever in Scripture. Today, these beliefs are prevalent within Christianity worldwide, and the ecumenical movement is seeking something upon which to unite all denominations. It is this type of coming together over beliefs held in common that will usher in the second coming of Christ. John wrote,

And I saw three unclean spirits like frogs coming out of the mouth of the dragon, out of the mouth of the beast, and out of the mouth of the false prophet. For they are spirits of demons, performing signs, which go out to the kings of the earth and of the whole world, to gather them to the battle of that great day of God Almighty.

"Behold, I [Jesus] am coming as a thief. Blessed is he who watches, and keeps his garments, lest he walk naked and they see his shame" (Revelation 16:13–15).

Chapter 5

Jesus Is Coming!

Jesus' words on this subject will give us the counsel we need to be ready for His second coming. Concerning what we have been studying, He gives this admonition: "Now when these things begin to happen, look up and lift up your heads, because your redemption draws near" (Luke 21:28). Without a doubt, we are living in the time when the signs of Jesus' coming are being fulfilled, so we need to be preparing for it, because it is very near. Christ offered these words of caution concerning His second coming: "Take heed that no one deceives you" (Matthew 24:4).

The only way to keep from being deceived is to know what the Bible says about the Second

Coming. At His ascension, Jesus gave a live demonstration of what His return will be like.

> Now when He [Jesus] had spoken these things, while they [the disciples] watched, He was taken up, and a cloud received Him out of their sight. And while they looked steadfastly toward heaven as He went up, behold, two men stood by them in white apparel, who also said, "Men of Galilee, why do you stand gazing up into heaven? This same Jesus, who was taken up from you into heaven, will so come in like manner as you saw Him go into heaven" (Acts 1:9–11).

"In like manner" means that just as the disciples saw Jesus go into heaven, we will see Him return from heaven. His coming will not be a secret or hidden. "Behold, He is coming with clouds, and every eye will see Him, even they who pierced Him. And all the tribes of the earth will mourn because of Him. Even so, Amen" (Revelation 1:7). Christ's own words are the clearest instruction we can receive. In describing His return, Jesus used the phrase "so also will the coming of the Son of

Man be", at least four times. This is what it will be like: "For as the lightning comes from the east and flashes to the west, so also will the coming of the Son of Man be" (Matthew 24:27).

I remember my father telling me one day, "If you will get things ready, tomorrow when I get home, we will go and spend the night fishing." Mother fixed us a basket of food, and I got all of our fishing gear ready. When we got to the river, Dad found a good spot, cut down some tree limbs, and made a lean-to where we could spend the night. The fish weren't biting, and I got sleepy, so I went and lay down. It wasn't long until I heard the rumble of thunder in the distance. As the lighting and thunder neared, Dad came and sat down beside me. The lightning would light up the night sky like it was daylight, and the thunder got progressively louder until it seemed to shake the ground. When the Bible compares Jesus' coming to the lightning that flashes across the entire night sky, you can be sure that you will be able to see Jesus when He returns.

Our Lord also compared His second coming to the days of Noah: "As the days of Noah were, so also will the coming of the Son of Man be. For as in the days before the flood, they were eating and drinking, marrying and giving in marriage, until the day that Noah entered the ark, and did not know until the flood came and took them all away, so also will the coming of the Son of Man be" (Matthew 24:37–39). What an accurate picture of our day! "Eating and drinking" consumes much of people's leisure time, with no thought of eternity or the consequences of sin. People are busy satisfying their lustful desires, even "marrying and giving in marriage" to partners of the same sex. Some of the saddest words spoken in Scripture are found in these verses—"and [they] did not know . . ." Multitudes, blinded by the cares of this life, do not know that Jesus' return is near, even "at the doors!" (verse 33).

Christ also taught that just before His return, men and women would be too preoccupied with the things of this life to be concerned with what was coming. "Likewise as it was also in the days of Lot: They ate, they drank, they bought, they sold, they planted, they built; but on the day that Lot went out of Sodom it rained fire and brimstone from heaven and destroyed them all. Even so will it be in the day when the Son of Man is revealed" (Luke 17:28–30). The comparisons are too obvious for us to ignore. The hour is late. Now is the time for each one of us to prepare for the coming the Lord and to be ready for His coming.

Many texts in the Bible refer to the glory that will attend the coming of Christ. "Then they will see the Son of Man coming in a cloud with power and great glory" (Luke 21:27). We are given insight into just how glorious His return will be. Jesus said, "Whoever is ashamed of Me and My words, of him the Son of Man will be ashamed when He comes in His own glory, and in His Father's, and of the holy angels" (Luke 9:26). Since Jesus is coming in His own glory, what is His glory like? "Now after six days Jesus took Peter, James, and John his brother, led them up on a high mountain by themselves; and He was transfigured before them. His face shone like the sun, and His clothes became as white as the light" (Matthew 17:1, 2). The glory shining from Jesus' face and clothing was so bright that Peter, James, and John fell to the ground. Throughout Christ's life, every time humanity glimpsed His glory, people either fell to the ground or drew back in fear. Imagine what it will be like when He comes in *all* of His glory!

Yet that's not all, for Jesus is also coming in His Father's glory. A good example of God's glory was when He spoke to the children of Israel from Mount Sinai. He told Moses to come up into the mountain and meet with Him there. On the mountain, God wrote the Ten Commandments on tablets of stone for the second time. During this meeting with the Lord, Moses made this daring request: "Please, show me Your glory" (Exodus 33:18). God replied, "No man shall see Me, and live" (verse 20). What a wonderful, compassionate, and caring Lord we have! "And the LORD said, 'Here is a place by Me, and you shall stand on the rock. So it shall be, while My glory passes by, that I will put you in the cleft of the rock, and will cover you with My hand while I pass by. Then I will take away My hand, and you shall see My back; but My face shall not be seen' " (verses 21–23). Looking at the back of God, Moses saw all the wonderful attributes of a loving Lord, for this is His glory (Exodus 34:5–7).

Leaving the mountain, Moses made his way back down to the camp of Israel, and on approaching the camp, Aaron and the elders came out to meet him. "So when Aaron and all the children of Israel saw Moses, behold, the skin of his face shone, and they were afraid to come near him. . . . And when Moses had finished speaking with them, he put a veil on his face" (verses 30, 33). If the reflected glory of God was so bright that Moses had to put a veil over his face so the people could look at him (verses 33–35), imagine what it will be like when Christ returns in His Father's glory!

Yet Jesus' coming will be even more glorious, for Scripture states that He is returning with the glory of the holy angels as well (see Luke 9:26). We find a wonderful example of the glory of angels at the resurrection of Christ. "And behold, there was a great earthquake; for an angel of the Lord descended from heaven, and came and rolled back the stone from the door, and sat on it. His countenance was like lightning, and his clothing as white as snow. And the guards shook for fear of him, and became like dead men" (Matthew 28:2–4). This is the glory of just one angel! When Jesus returns, *all* the angels of heaven are coming with Him. "When the Son of Man comes in His glory, and all the holy angels with Him, then He will sit on the throne of His glory" (Matthew 25:31). Scripture doesn't number the angels, but it speaks of them in one text as "an innumerable company" (Hebrews 12:22), and in another, it describes them as "the armies in heaven" (Revelation 19:14).

In the book of Revelation, the apostle John gives us the closest approximation of the number of angels: "Then I looked, and I heard the voice of many angels around the throne, the living creatures, and the elders; and the number of them was ten thousand times ten thousand, and thousands of thousands" (Revelation 5:11). "Ten thousand times ten thousand" is one hundred million, yet there are more than that, because John adds, "and thousands of thousands." Imagine what it will be like when more than one hundred million angels come, and each one's countenance is like lightning. This glory will light up the sky for the entire world, and every eye will see Jesus (Revelation 1:7). With the sound of a trumpet (Isaiah 18:3), His words will roll through this earth like peals of the loudest thunder, and all the dead who have died in faith will come forth from the grave. "Then we who are alive and remain shall be caught up together with them in the clouds to meet the Lord in the air" (1 Thessalonians 4:17). Christ will then say to the redeemed from all ages, "Come, you blessed of My Father, inherit the kingdom prepared for you from the foundation of the world" (Matthew 25:34).

The Bible describes the second coming of Christ in this manner, and considering the signs of His return that are occurring today, we need to be strong in the faith, knowing that Christ will keep His word. "Let not your heart be troubled; you believe in God, believe also in Me. In My Father's house are many mansions; if it were not so, I would have told you. I go to prepare a place for you. And if I go and prepare a place for you, I will come again and receive you to Myself; that where I am, there you may be also" (John 14:1–3).

FREE Lessons at www.BibleStudies.com

Call:
1-888-456-7933

Write:
Discover
P.O. Box 999
Loveland, CO 80539

It's easy to learn more about the Bible!